STARS AND PLANETS

Marcus Chown

Macdonald Educational

How to use this book

First, look at the contents page opposite. Read the chapter list to see if it includes the subject you want. The list tells you what each page is about. You can then find the page with the information you need.

If you want to know about one particular thing, look it up in the index on page 31. For example, if you want to know about comets, the index tells you that there is something about them on page 17. The index also lists the pictures in the book.

When you read this book, you will find some unusual words. The glossary on page 30 explains what they mean.

Series Editor
Margaret Conroy

Book Editor
Peter Harrison

Factual Adviser
John Griffiths

Reading Consultant
Amy Gibbs

Series Design
Robert Mathias/Anne Isseyegh

Book Design
Julia Osorno

Production
Marguerite Fenn

Picture Research
Kathy Lockley

Teacher Panel
John Allen, Bernadette Hill, Hazel Stimpson

Illustrations
Robert Burns 8–9, 10–11, 16–17, 24–25
Jerry Collins Front cover
Julia Osorno 8–9, 14–15, 28–29
Kate Rogers 22, 26–27

Photographs
Aldus Archive: 22–23
Michael Holford: 29
Pictorial Press: 12
Robin Scagell: Cover
Science Photo Library: 7, 13T, 14–15, 17, 18–19T, 18–19B, 20, 21T, 23T, 27
ZEFA: 14B, 21B

CONTENTS

OUR PLANET

The Earth

We live on a ball of rock, measuring about 13,000 kilometres across, which we call the planet Earth. We cannot float off into space because the Earth pulls us down fiercely with a force which we call gravity. This is one of the forces which holds the world together.

The air we breathe and the water we drink come from a misty layer of gases which we call the atmosphere, wrapped tightly around the world, and held there by gravity.

The Earth's atmosphere is what made it possible for life to develop on Earth, but although the atmosphere is so important it does not stretch very far above us. Imagine the Earth is the size of an apple. The atmosphere would only be as thick as the skin on the apple.

We live on dry land which is part of the Earth's cool outer surface, or crust. We live on only one quarter of the Earth's rocky crust; the rest is under the sea. Below the Earth's crust lies what we call the mantle, made of rocks so hot they have melted. Some parts of the crust are thicker than others; the thinnest parts are only 10 kilometres thick.

Nothing in the Universe can escape the pull of gravity. The gravity of the Earth plucks apples from trees and keeps the Moon circling the Earth in space for ever.

The Space Shuttle in orbit above the Earth. The clouds are part of the atmosphere, and space appears black.

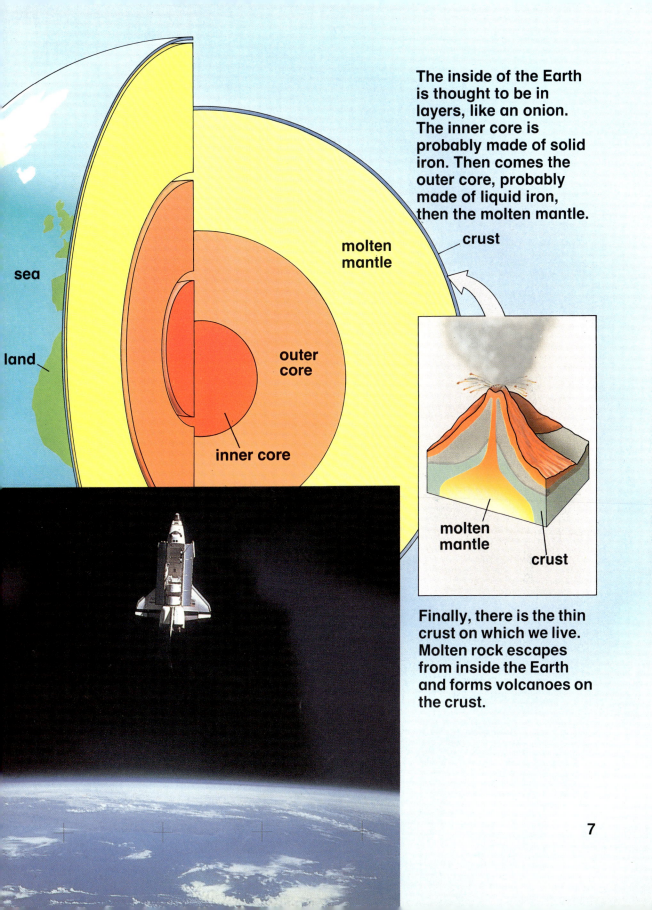

The inside of the Earth is thought to be in layers, like an onion. The inner core is probably made of solid iron. Then comes the outer core, probably made of liquid iron, then the molten mantle.

sea

land

molten mantle

crust

outer core

inner core

molten mantle

crust

Finally, there is the thin crust on which we live. Molten rock escapes from inside the Earth and forms volcanoes on the crust.

The Earth in orbit

The seasons: when the northern hemisphere is tipped towards the Sun, people who live there get the full warming effect of the Sun; they have summer. Half a year later, when the northern hemisphere is tipped away from the Sun, they have winter. The Sun keeps lands which are nearer the Equator warm the whole year round.

Have you ever watched a spinning top? The outside whizzes around very fast, but there is a tiny spot at the top and bottom which seems to stay very still. The Earth spins like that. At the top and bottom, which we call the North and South Poles, people are hardly moving at all. At the Equator, around the middle of the Earth, people are moving without knowing it at 1,700 kilometres per hour.

The Earth spins around a line through its North and South Poles called an axis. It takes 24 hours to spin on its axis, and that is why our day is 24 hours long.

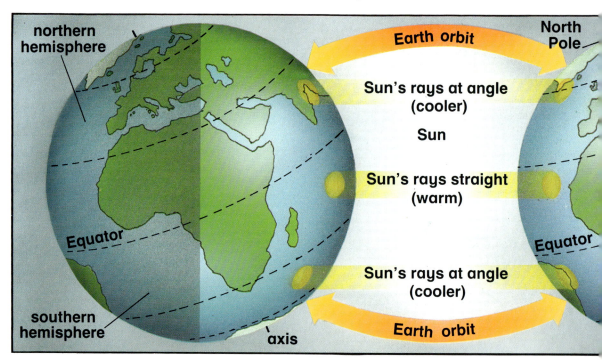

northern hemisphere
Earth orbit
North Pole
Sun's rays at angle (cooler)
Sun
Sun's rays straight (warm)
Equator
Equator
Sun's rays at angle (cooler)
southern hemisphere
axis
Earth orbit

Now look at a globe and find where the Equator is drawn. The line divides the globe into two halves, or hemispheres, the northern hemisphere, and the southern.
The Earth does not spin upright, but at a tilt. We have spring, summer, autumn and winter, because the two hemispheres are tipped towards the Sun at different times of the year.

The Sun is about 150 million kilometres away from the Earth. But because it is so huge in comparison, the Sun's gravity holds the Earth and keeps it moving in a path, or orbit, which is slightly oval in shape. So, at certain times the Earth is closer to the Sun than at others. It takes the Earth 365 days to orbit the Sun, and this is why our year is 365 days long.

Ancient peoples, like the Aztecs of Mexico, made calendars by observing the Sun, and gave the days of the month special symbols.

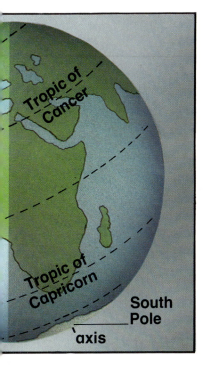

Tropic of Cancer

Tropic of Capricorn

South Pole

axis

Flower

Deer

Rain

Reed

The Moon

On the Earth's endless journeys around the Sun it takes its own small companion, the Moon, with it. The Sun is bigger than the Earth, and so the Earth is held by the pull of its gravity. But the Earth is 81 times bigger than the Moon, and so the Moon is also held by the pull of the Earth. It circles the Earth every 27 days, a period of time we call a month.

The Moon is a small, dead, world, no longer hot and molten inside like the Earth. It cooled down long ago and now has no atmosphere to protect it from the huge pieces of rubble called meteorites which bombard it from space. Because there is no atmosphere, the Moon has no wind. Astronauts on the Moon must carry their own air, and their footprints last because no wind disturbs them.

The Moon's gravity pulls on our planet and creates tides. On the near side, it pulls the sea away from the Earth. On the far side, it pulls the Earth away from the sea. This makes two bulges in the oceans, on opposite sides of the Earth. As the Earth turns beneath the Moon these bulges move making the sea level rise and fall twice every 24 hours.

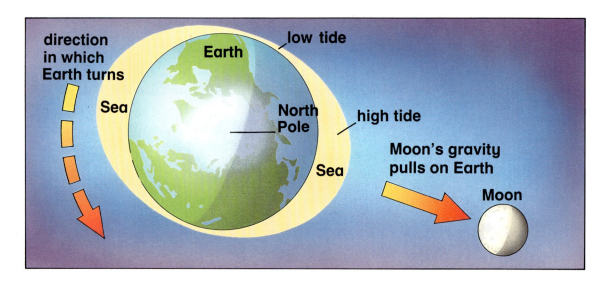

direction in which Earth turns

low tide

Earth

Sea

North Pole

high tide

Sea

Moon's gravity pulls on Earth

Moon

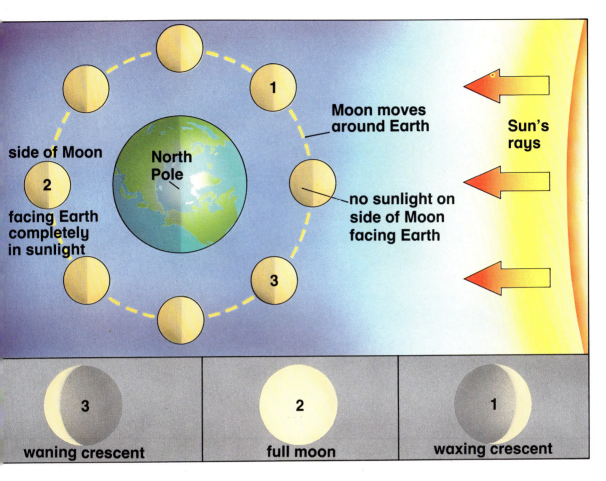

side of Moon

North Pole

2

facing Earth completely in sunlight

Moon moves around Earth

no sunlight on side of Moon facing Earth

Sun's rays

1

3

3	2	1
waning crescent	full moon	waxing crescent

Because the Moon is so small, its gravity is weak. On the Moon's surface astronauts weigh only one-sixth as much as on Earth, and can long-jump six times as far.

We can still feel the effect of the Moon's gravity on Earth, even though it is weak. When the Moon passes over the seas, water surges towards the Moon. The Sun's gravity, too, pulls the Earth's seas towards it. The Sun is so far away it has less effect. Without the Moon we would have lower tides.

In the course of a month, more and more sunlight falls on the side of the Moon facing the Earth. First the face is dark, then it becomes a crescent moon. Then, when the whole face is in sunlight, we have a full moon. Then the light fades, the 'waning crescent', and finally the face is completely dark once more.

Looking at the sky

Scientists whose job it is to look at stars and planets are called astronomers. They need powerful telescopes to watch the night sky. A telescope must do two things. First, it must be big enough to collect a lot of light from stars which shine too dimly for the human eye to see. Secondly, it must be able to show tiny details, like the mountains on the Moon, or the rings around the planet Saturn.

All warm objects give off invisible light called infra-red. Special detectors can pick up this invisible light, and show us what our eyes cannot see. This picture shows us more of the Orion Nebula than we could see with our eyes.

Even the huge modern telescopes which astronomers now use have difficulty in looking through the Earth's murky atmosphere. Astronomers want to see more, and they now have plans for a telescope in space, called the Hubble Space Telescope. This will orbit above our atmosphere, and allow us to 'see' into space more clearly.

This infra-red photograph shows which parts of a house are giving out most heat. Heat gives out infra-red, so the brightest parts of the picture are where heat is escaping from the house into the air.

This normal picture of a house is taken in visible light, the sort which our eyes can see. But recently people have made kinds of detectors which see other sorts of light, from infra-red to X-rays.

For thousands of years people have studied the light of the stars. But now we know that there are other sorts of radiation coming from the stars which are invisible to human eyes.

For instance, we know that even very cold stars give out infra-red light, and very hot ones X-rays. Modern telescopes can pick up these invisible rays, and astronomers can now learn about things they cannot see directly.

AROUND THE SUN

The Sun

The Sun is a hot glowing ball about a million kilometres across. Its surface is not solid like Earth's because it is made of gas, like the air we breathe. But it burns more hotly than any fire because hydrogen works deep in its heart.

Hydrogen can be much more powerful than fuels like oil and coal which we use to heat our homes. This is because it can be a nuclear fuel, the stuff of nuclear bombs. The Sun's nuclear fuel has kept it burning for about 5,000 million years, and will keep it burning for many years more.

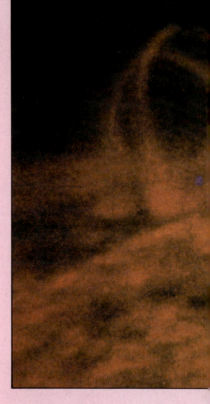

We can take pictures of the Sun's ultra-violet light. The bright loop is a stream of hot gas which the Sun has flung into space.

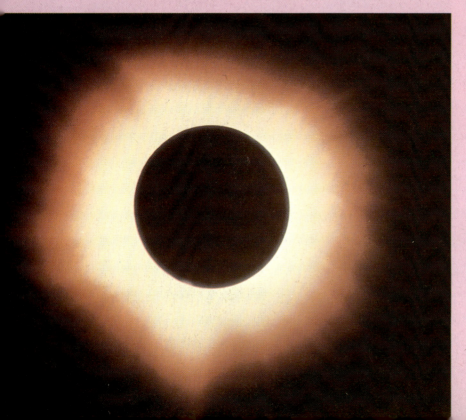

The Sun's atmosphere, or corona, can also be looked at through an instrument called a coronagraph.

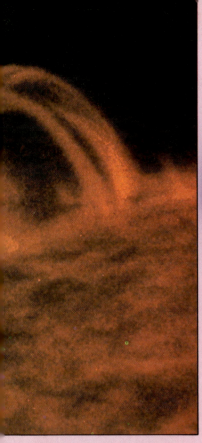

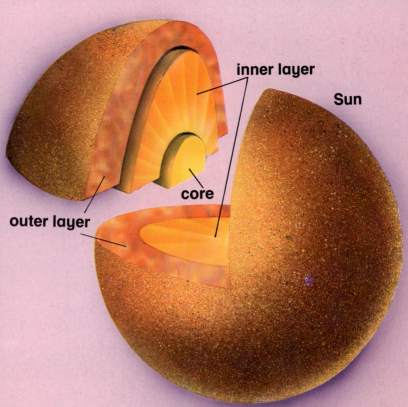

inner layer

Sun

core

outer layer

The Sun provides the light and heat which makes life on Earth possible. Without it, ours would be a cold, dark world. If it were not in the sky our night would last for ever, and summer would turn to winter. But the Sun can also be harmful to life; the Sun's ultra-violet light can cause painful sunburn.

Although the Sun looks round and compact in our sky, its thin atmosphere streams invisibly out into space for millions of miles. We can only see it clearly during a total eclipse of the Sun, when the Moon passes between the Earth and the Sun, and blots out the Sun's light. The Sun's outer atmosphere, the solar wind, blows to the Earth and beyond.

At the centre of the Sun nuclear fuel is being turned into heat which takes about a million years to work its way from the centre to the surface of the Sun. Some of this heat escapes across space to warm the Earth.

15

The Solar System

The Earth is one of nine planets which circle the Sun and make up the Solar System. You can see the five nearest planets, Mercury, Venus, Mars, Jupiter and Saturn on clear nights if you know where to look. But you will need a telescope to see the other planets Uranus, Neptune and Pluto. Pluto is so faint that it was not noticed until this century.

All the planets move in a narrow band of sky called the zodiac. Ancient peoples knew that planets behave differently from stars. Planets are near and it is easy to spot them moving. But the stars are so far away that they do not look as though they are moving. The 12 groups of 'fixed' stars in the zodiac all have names given to them long ago by the astronomers of the past.

The nine planets of the Solar System all move around the Sun in regular paths, or orbits. There is a belt of asteroids, part of the rubble in the Solar System, betwen Mars and Jupiter.

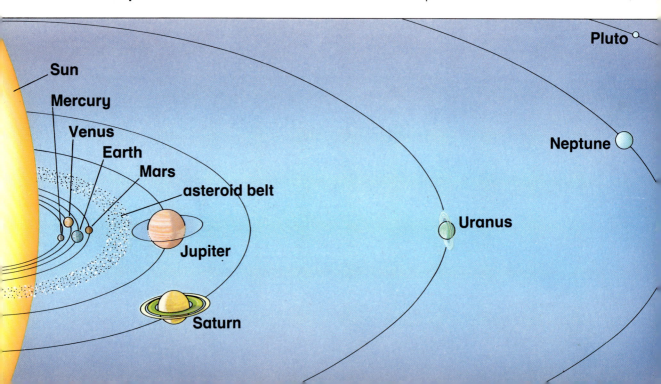

Sun
Mercury
Venus
Earth
Mars
asteroid belt
Jupiter
Saturn
Uranus
Neptune
Pluto

Beta Pictoris is a star 50 light years from the Sun. In 1983, an Earth satellite found that the star was giving out a lot of infra-red light. Astronomers now know that the extra light is coming from dust circling the star, and think we may be seeing another Solar System being born.

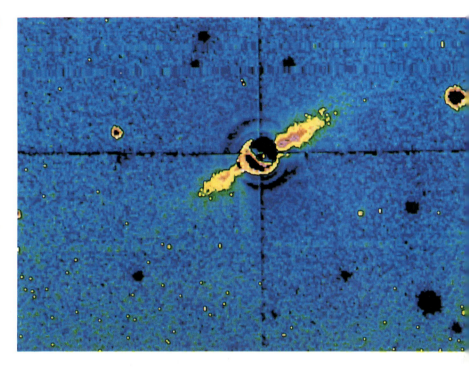

The two planets closest to the Sun are much hotter than Earth. Mercury is nearest, but Venus, the second planet, is hotter because its thick atmosphere traps the Sun's rays, and heats it up like a greenhouse. These are the only planets without moons.

Pluto, the farthest planet, is a dead, dark world where the Sun's heat and light scarcely reach. But there are other strange, cold travellers in the Solar System. Comets look rather like snowballs a few kilometres across. We can see their bright tails when they travel near the Sun. The Solar System contains a lot of rubble too, mostly dust. Specks of this dust strike the Earth's atmosphere and leave streaks of light, or meteors, in the sky.

The Sun is 109 times bigger than the Earth, and contains most of the material in the Solar System. The giant planets Jupiter and Saturn contain most of the rest.

ercury Venus Earth Mars

Jupiter

_____ **Sun**

17

Space probes

A space probe is a space craft without people on board. It can fly to a planet and find out what it is like close up, and send the information back to us on Earth. Probes can measure how hot a planet's surface is, or take photographs telling us how a planet looks.

The probes are launched into space by rockets and controlled by people back on Earth. Today, probes have visited all the Solar System planets except the two furthest, Neptune and Pluto.

Space probes have dropped landers on the surface of the Moon, Venus and Mars. The Soviet Venera landers floated on their parachutes down through the poisonous clouds of Venus, but the heat on the surface melted the landers, and in hours they stopped sending back pictures. American Viking landers took photographs from the surface of Mars and looked for signs of life ten years ago. Scientists are still arguing about whether or not Viking did find signs of life.

Planets have not been the only target of space probes. In 1986, a total of five probes, including Europe's Giotto, met Halley's Comet as it swung around the Sun in its 76-year orbit. It will take scientists many years to examine what they found.

A model of the Voyager space probe being checked before its launch. Rockets took both probes into space in 1977. Both probes flew past the planets Jupiter and Saturn. Voyager 2 photographed Uranus too, and is due to reach Neptune in 1989.

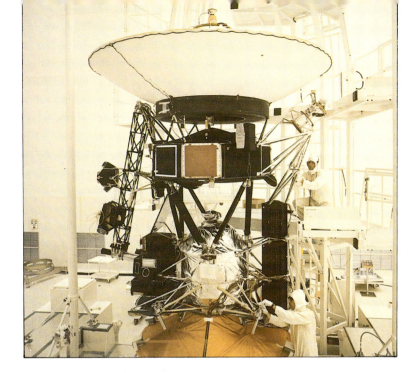

Venus is the planet closest to the Earth and the one nearest in size. The Pioneer probes arrived there in 1978. They orbited the planet, and found volcanoes and valleys much larger than any on Earth, and lightning storms high in the clouds.

Planets in view

The Voyager space probes flew past the planet Saturn in 1980 and 1981. Saturn is about nine times bigger than the Earth, and is also wrapped in clouds. Large rings, mostly of ice, surround the planet. Scientists think that the ice is kept together by the gravity of tiny 'shepherd' moons holding the ice like a shepherd keeping sheep together. Astronomers have seen 22 other large moons around Saturn. Titan is the largest.

Jupiter is 11 times the size of the Earth, and the largest of all the planets. In 1979, the American space probes, Voyager 1 and Voyager 2, flew past it and took the clearest pictures yet of the cloudy planet.

Both Voyager probes have photographed Saturn, its moons and its beautiful rings. Titan, the largest of the moons, has a thick atmosphere of its own, of orange fog.

Red and orange clouds sweep around Jupiter once every ten hours as it turns. Two of Jupiter's moons can be seen in this picture, one looking like an orange dot against the clouds.

Among the clouds on Jupiter is the Great Red Spot, which alone is bigger than the Earth. Astronomers think it is a storm which has been raging on Jupiter for many years.

Jupiter has 16 known moons. The four biggest are Io, Callisto, Ganymede and Europa. The Voyager space probes also found a thin ring of rubble circling Jupiter.

The Voyager probes came quite close to some of Jupiter's moons. Europa, one of the four biggest, is covered in ice, and there are at least six active volcanoes on Io's surface. If Jupiter had been a little bigger, its own heat would have made it shine, and turned it into a Sun.

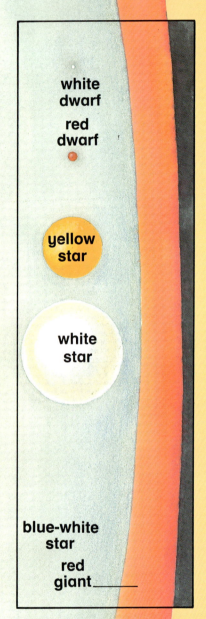

white
dwarf

red
dwarf

yellow
star

white
star

blue-white
star

red
giant

THE STARS

What are stars?

Stars are huge balls of hot, glowing gas just like our own Sun. Our Sun is a yellow star, but it is easy to see stars which are other colours, such as red and white, in the sky.

A star's colour tells you how hot it is. The coolest stars are a dull cherry-red colour, like coals which have nearly burned out. Brilliant blue-white stars, like hot coals, are hottest, and are also usually the youngest and most massive. Other stars, called white dwarfs, are only as big as the Earth.

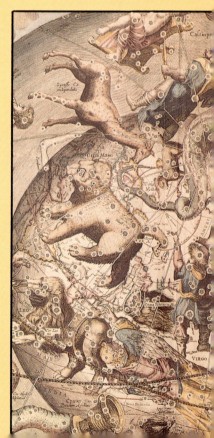

Stars are many sizes, from white dwarfs no bigger than the Earth, to vast red giants.

Orion is one of the brightest groups of stars in the sky, and one of the easiest to remember. The three stars of the belt are all very young, hot stars and are among the most luminous we can see.

From the earliest times, people have grouped stars together into constellations and imagined human and animal figures among them. These figures were drawn by the 17th century map-maker Andreas Cellerius.

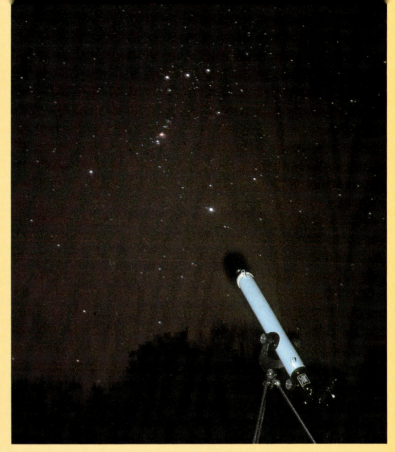

Some stars, called red giants, are so big that one could swallow the Sun and the planets as far as Mars. But even these stars appear only as tiny specks of light because they are so far away. Alpha Centauri, our nearest star, is so distant that its light takes four and a half years to reach us. A Voyager probe would take 80,000 years to travel there.

Kilometres are useless for measuring the huge distances between stars, because there are so many noughts when you write them down! So astronomers talk about light years instead: the distance light travels in a year, which is 10 trillion kilometres. So we talk about Alpha Centauri being four and a half light years away.

Stars as signs

We can see about 6,000 stars with the naked eye. People have known for thousands of years that the stars do not seem to move in the sky from month to month like the planets. To help them remember the important ones, they have imagined that there are patterns in the stars. They have given names to different groups, or constellations, of stars. For example, there is a constellation of stars which can be seen in our skies which people once thought looked like a bear. Astronomers call it Ursa Major, or the Great Bear.

In prehistoric times, and in the present, wandering peoples found that the stars helped them to find their way.

The group of stars known as the Plough is very useful for finding where north is. But first you must find the two stars in the Plough which are known as the 'pointer' stars. An imaginary line through them points to Polaris, the Pole Star, which hangs right above the Earth's North Pole.

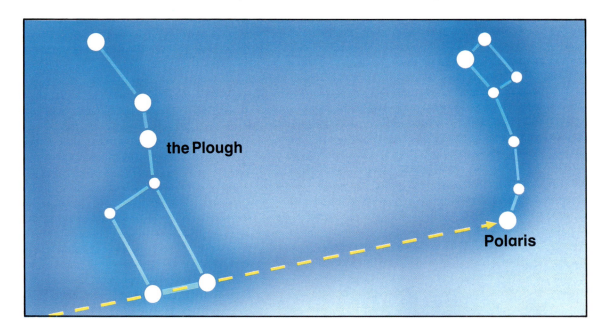

the Plough

Polaris

In the northern hemisphere, there is a star known as the Pole Star, or Polaris. If we travel towards it, we are travelling north. The Pole Star can be found by using two stars in the Great Bear which point to it.

Zodiac constellations are in the same band of sky as the planets, and so are important to remember, which is why ancient peoples imagined patterns around them like this figure, Aquarius the water carrier. This constellation is visible from the southern hemisphere.

The stars also helped people to tell the time of the year. The constellations which can be seen from any place on Earth change from season to season, and so a farmer can know from the stars when it is time to plant seeds or harvest crops. For example, the star Sirius was very important to the ancient Egyptians, because they knew that when Sirius first appeared in the sky it was the time of the year when the river Nile would flood.

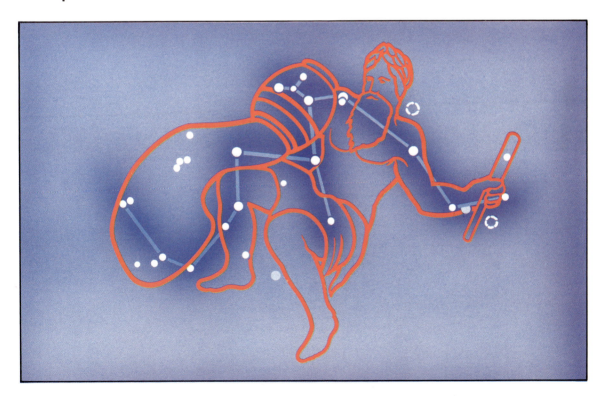

GALAXIES

The Milky Way

Our Sun is one of a hundred thousand million other stars which make up the Milky Way, a giant whirlpool of stars 100,000 light years across. On a clear summer's night, the Milky Way appears as a misty band of light in the sky. The crowds of stars there are so thick and far away that they blur into each other. Clouds of dust in space make the shape of the Milky Way difficult to see. However dust cannot blot out the invisible rays we call radio waves, so astronomers have been able to use radio telescopes to find out that the Milky Way is shaped like a spiral.

There are many, many other galaxies in the Universe, some bigger, some smaller, others the same size as our own. Some are spiral galaxies, like ours, but others, called elliptical galaxies, are more oval or round in shape. Astronomers think that spiral galaxies were spinning fast when they formed, and that elliptical galaxies were spinning slowly.

The stars in each galaxy are held together by the force of gravity. Each star has its own fixed path around the centre. It takes 230 million years for the Sun to circle once around the centre of the Milky Way.

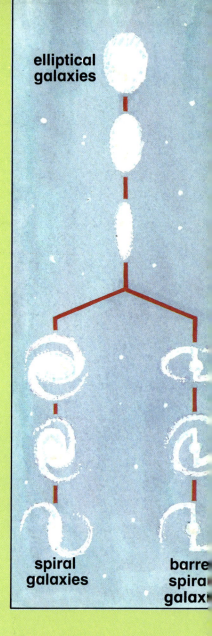

elliptical galaxies

spiral galaxies

barre spira galax

Galaxies come in only a few shapes. The astronomer Edwin Hubble found that most galaxies are either ellipticals or spirals.

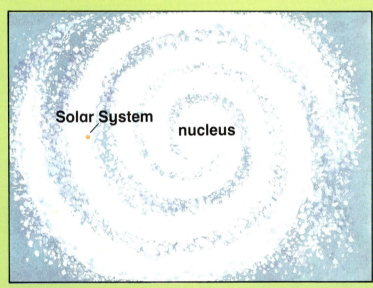

Astronomers call this galaxy M81. It looks very much as our own Milky Way would look if we could see it from outside. The blue stars along the spiral arms are the youngest ones, the red ones are older.

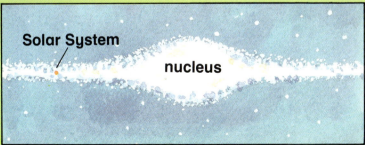

The Sun and Solar System are in a spiral arm of the Milky Way about two-thirds of the way out from the centre, or nucleus. This is most easily seen if the spiral of the Galaxy is looked at from above. From the side, the Galaxy's spiral arms are less visible.

First and last

The whole Universe is expanding. Every galaxy, including our own Milky Way, is rushing away from every other galaxy at a very high speed.

Astronomers used to think that the Universe had been expanding for ever, and that new matter was constantly appearing to fill the gaps between the galaxies. They called this the Steady State Theory and said the Universe had no beginning.

Now astronomers think that about 15 billion years ago there was an enormous explosion which gave birth to the Universe. They call this explanation the Big Bang Theory. According to the Big Bang Theory, all the matter in the Universe exploded from a point, and has been expanding and cooling down ever since.

The Universe suddenly came into existence 15 billion years ago in the Big Bang. From that time on, the Universe has been expanding and cooling. When the Big Bang happened, matter was squeezed very tightly together and was very hot indeed.

This rock painting comes from Easter Island. The islanders believed that the world hatched from an egg like the one the man is holding. This is not so very different from astronomers' modern Big Bang idea.

The Big Bang Theory explains something the Steady State Theory cannot account for. Wherever astronomers look in the sky, they see radio waves. They call this cosmic background radiation, and they are pretty sure that it is the remains of the explosion from the Big Bang. So the Big Bang probably did happen, although, at the moment, no-one knows what happened before.

The ancient Egyptians believed that the goddess Nut gave birth to the Universe, and that her body enclosed the world.

GLOSSARY, BOOKS TO READ

A glossary is a word list. This one explains unusual words that are used in this book.

Astronomer A scientist whose job it is to look at the stars and planets around us.

Atmosphere The thin layer of gas which surrounds a planet or star.

Axis The line around which something spins or rotates.

Comet A lump of ice and dust which grows a tail when its orbit takes it near the Sun.

Constellation A group of stars which people have given a name.

Equator A line which people have imagined dividing the Earth into two halves.

Galaxy A giant island of stars, like our own Milky Way.

Gravity A force which makes every object in the Universe pull on every other object.

Hydrogen The lightest gas, and the substance most of the Universe is made of.

Infra-red Invisible light given out by any warm object.

Mantle The region of the Earth below the crust where the rocks have melted.

Meteor The streak of light made by a speck of space dust burning up as it falls into the Earth's atmosphere.

Meteorite A speck of space dust which reaches the Earth's surface.

Nuclear Energy Energy from inside atoms.

Orbit The path gravity forces one body to take around another.

Planet A body, like the Earth, which does not produce its own heat.

Pole The points at the top or bottom of the Earth through which the axis passes.

Radiation The visible and invisible light which flows to us across space.

Star A body, like the Sun, which produces its own heat and light.

Telescope An instrument which people use to make distant objects look closer.

Ultra-violet Radiation from hot objects which causes sunburn.

Volcano A break in the Earth's crust where the hot mantle spills out.

X-ray A type of invisible light given out by only the hottest bodies in the Universe.

Zodiac The band of the sky in which we can see the planets.

BOOKS TO READ
The Young Astronomer's Handbook by Ian Ridpath, Hamlyn 1981.
Space Scientist (a series of books) by Heather Couper, Franklin Watts, 1985.
Our Planet (My First Encyclopaedia, volume 6) by Susan Baker, Macdonald 1982.
Just Look At . . . The Universe by Neil Ardley, Macdonald 1985
The Young Astronomer by Sheila Snowden, Usborne 1983.
The Spotters' Guide to the Night Sky by Nigel Henbest, Usborne 1979.